Life on the Edge

A Successful Family Resource Guide

Teacher Edition

Dr. Creflo A. Dollar and Taffi L. Dollar

Other Resource Guides in *The Successful Family* Series

Before the Ring
Marriage Enhancement
Family Planning and Children
The Secret to a Happy Family
Making a Go of It

Life on the Edge: Resource Guide – Teacher Guide
ISBN 1-59089-710-2
Copyright © 2002 by Dr. Creflo A. Dollar and Taffi L. Dollar

Published by:
Creflo Dollar Ministries
P.O. Box 490124
College Park, GA 30349

CONTENTS

HOW TO USE THIS RESOURCE GUIDE

Family counseling sessions, whether in a Christian or secular environment, usually transform themselves into unproductive and intensely dramatic scenes. These sessions often erupt into ugly displays of pent-up emotion where the "patients" indulge in bouts of name-calling and finger pointing. As a result, more time is spent discussing the problem than finding a long-lasting solution.

This resource guide is designed to be used in conjunction with *Part VI: Life on the Edge*, of *The Successful Family* reference book. Your goal as an instructor or facilitator is to show group members how to apply the principles in the book to their everyday lives. The exercises and in-depth information presented in this resource guide will assist you in creating an interesting and enjoyable class setting. As members focus on and implement the solutions to their problems, they will mature in those areas of their lives in which they are weak.

There is no right or wrong way to use this guide. Depending on the exercise, you may want students to work alone, with a partner or in a group. However, be sure to allow them enough time to review the relevant chapters and complete the corresponding exercises. Encouragement and motivation from you will enable group members to overcome the desire to give up and quit when presented with a challenge.

The time you spend preparing for your class is critical to the group's success. Follow these steps to prepare for each exercise:

- Pray for wisdom.
- Read the corresponding chapter(s) in part six of *The Successful Family*.
- Be creative when developing lesson plans. If necessary, incorporate additional outside material. Ensure that they meet the needs of everyone involved.
- Allow enough time for the material to be thoroughly covered before moving on to the next exercise.

Invite group members to share their own experiences through class discussions. Be sure to refrain from dominating this time by expressing your personal views. Instead, allow members the opportunity to share what is in their hearts. Create a safe and inviting atmosphere by being sensitive to their feelings, valuing their responses and maintaining focus and control of the group. Last, but not least, don't forget to encourage members to enjoy the journey to successful, vibrant relationships!

MY COMMITMENT

If you are fed up with failed relationships and are serious about seeing change take place in your life, read the following statements, and then sign your name at the bottom of this page. Make time in your daily schedule to give voice to your commitment to change so that you can remain focused.

- I will read *Part VI: Life on the Edge*, of *The Successful Family* and complete the corresponding exercises. If this is a group session, and I must miss a meeting, I will make up all missed assignments.

- I will designate a specific time frame daily in which to study the information and complete the exercises.

- If this is a group, I will be on time for each session. I realize that my tardiness is a distraction to others and causes me to miss out on valuable information.

- I will share my answers with a trusted friend and/or participate in group discussions.

- I will be honest with myself and/or other group members.

- I commit to love myself enough to successfully complete this session no matter how difficult or challenging the exercises seem.

- I will apply what I learn and periodically gauge my growth.

- I commit to confidentiality and will not discuss the personal affairs of others outside of the group.

_____   _____
Signature   Date

Exercise One:

FISTS OF FURY

Talk About It!

Using chapter 32, Domestic Violence, as a guide, review the dynamics and dangers of spousal abuse. Emphasize the importance of prevention and intervention, and how denial can exacerbate the problem.

Abuse is "the maltreatment of any person in a family or a close personal relationship." This can include physical, verbal and sexual assault or threats of assault or death. Violent acts against individuals are most often committed by someone they know and trust, such as a spouse, parent, friend or significant other.

There are a variety of reasons as to why one person would abuse another. Use this exercise to identify the "red flags" that are common among abusers.

- Good at disguising abusive behavior
- Seeks to control partner and punishes partner for resisting his/her control
- Acts impulsively
- Distrusts others

- Exhibits jealous behavior
- Ridicules, insults, minimizes or ignores partner's beliefs, principles, opinions or feelings
- Manipulates with lies or guilt
- Subjects partner to reckless driving
- Exhibits cruelty to animals and children
- Maintains control of finances or automobile(s)
- Humiliates partner in private and in public
- Insults or speaks badly of partner's family, effectively driving them away
- Withholds approval, appreciation or affection as punishment
- Shows force during arguments (hitting, shoving, slapping, pinching, choking, throwing objects, hitting walls, etc.)
- Exhibits a frightening rage
- Isolates partner
- Has unrealistic expectations
- Expects partner to dress in a specific manner
- Rapes partner
- Forces partner to watch pornographic videos or watch/participate in sexually degrading acts
- Threatens to commit suicide or kill partner if partner leaves
- Blames others (including partner) for his/her problems and feelings
- Minimizes, justifies or ignores violent behavior
- Threatens violence

Exercise Two:

THE CYCLE OF VIOLENCE

Abuse is a never-ending cycle; it only gets worse over time. Study the table below which details the phases of domestic violence.

Phase 1: Tension-Building

Abuser gets angry; increase in aggressive behavior (usually toward objects); breakdown in communication; increase in verbal and minor physical abuse; abuser places unrealistic/greater demands on the victim; abuser attempts to isolate partner from family/friends; victim tries to appease abuser; victim feels as if he/she is walking on eggshells; frequent arguments; abuser expresses feelings of hostility, tension and dissatisfaction.

Phase 3: The "Honeymoon"

The abuser: acts like the abuse did not happen; is apologetic (gives hope for change); promises not to hit the victim again; may blame the victim for the onset of violence; promise to get help; give gifts; become emotionally close to the victim; becomes generous, loving and helpful; expresses a genuine interest in the welfare of the victim; begs for forgiveness.

Phase 2: Acute Battering Incident

Severe physical abuse directed toward the victim: punching, biting, tripping, kicking, pinching, shoving, pushing, choking, slapping, hitting, use of objects/weapons; sexual abuse/spousal rape; verbal/emotional abuse; threats to life of victim/children.

Signs of Changed Behavior

Most victims of domestic violence have heard their abusers' promises to change; however, after repeated beatings, they know these promises are lies and find it difficult, if not impossible, to believe in them. However, a genuine change is possible if the abuser recognizes that he or she has a problem and makes an effort to change by receiving counseling.

The following is a list of positive signs to look for. Victims should exhibit caution until they witness a complete change in the abuser.

Change has occurred when he/she:

- Stops being violent or ceases to threaten you and others
- Acknowledges that violence is wrong
- Takes full responsibility for his/her behavior (without justifying it)
- Understands he/she has no right to control you.
- Does not try to control you
- Does not force you to have sex
- Allows you to express emotions without fear or feelings of intimidation
- Respects your opinion even if he/she does not agree
- Doesn't force his/her opinion upon you
- Respects your right to say "no"

This exercise will help you to develop a practical and effective safety plan for you and your children. You must be wise to protect your greatest asset—life.

Talk About It!

The purpose of this exercise is to explain how a safety plan can assist those who are victims of domestic violence in escaping from the next life-threatening situation. Discuss each statement. For more information, refer to pages 348-350 of *The Successful Family*.

Encourage group members who have never experienced abuse to place themselves in the victim's shoes and devise a detailed escape plan. Have all group members to share their plans aloud. Look for "holes"—areas that need strengthening—and offer suggestions on how they can do so. For those members who know someone being abused, encourage them to share this information with him or her.

---

1.   **Decide *how* to get out.**

- Decide where to go if you have to leave at night (public places that are open 24 hours, police or fire stations or the house of a trusted friend)

- Memorize the routes to the subway station, bus stop or train station nearest your home.

- Keep your purse and keys in a safe and easily accessible place in case you need to leave quickly.

- If you leave by car, be sure that you lock the doors immediately once inside.

- Be sure to have some cash on hand.

- Develop an escape plan from each room in your house.

- Know which doors of your home can be locked from within.

- If you live on the second floor or a higher level, create a plan that will allow you to escape safely (via fire escape or emergency stairwell)

2. **Communicate with someone you trust.**

- Think of a code word or phrase to use on the telephone with a friend to let him or her know you are in trouble. Tell your friend that when you say, "_____," it means you need them to call for help.

- Tell your neighbors to call the police if they hear suspicious noises, such as screaming, loud pounding against the walls or objects breaking.

- If you don't have a car, find a safe place where a friend can pick you up at any time. Know the locations of pay phones or local business that will allow you to use their phones to make a call.

- If a friend is not available during the crisis, call the National Domestic Violence Hotline at 1-800-799-SAFE. Memorize this telephone number, because this organization will immediately direct you to a safe alternative.

3. **Keep the children safe.**

- Make sure your children know how to dial 911 for any emergency.

- Teach them how to call the local police or fire department.

- Make sure they know how to escape during an emergency.

In addition, after you have left the abuser, be sure to contact local authorities and report any of the following behaviors he/she may exhibit.

- Attempts to find you after you have left
- Attempts to take away the children
- Threatens to harm you or the children
- Stalks you

Exercise Four:

PAINTING A TRUTHFUL PICTURE

Using chapter 32 of *The Successful Family* as a guide, complete the following sentences. When you are finished, compare your answers with the answer key at the back of this guide.

1.   Abuse is the _____ within a family or close personal relationship.

2.   Abuse is _____ the victim's fault.

3.   What are the three phases in the cycle of abuse?

_____

_____

_____

4.   List five reasons why victims remain in abusive situations.

_____

_____

_____

5.   Children of domestic violence generally mature into _____ or _____ themselves, beginning as early as their _____ years.

Talk About It!

Discussion the answers below. Be prepared to answer any additional questions.

1.   Maltreatment of any person

This can include physical, verbal and sexual abuse or threats of assault and death.

2.   Never

No one asks for, or enjoys, being physically, verbally or sexually assaulted by someone claiming to love him or her. The psychological and emotional problems of the abuser do not justify his or her explosive and uncontrolled burst of violence toward another person.

3.   Tension-building, acute battering incident, honeymoon stage

4.   *(Any five of the following will suffice)*

Fear the abuser will become more violent; fear their lives or the lives of their children are in jeopardy; rationalize that the abuse is due to external problems such as alcohol, drugs and work-related stress; hope for better times, since the abuser does not hit all the time; lack of support from family, friends, clergy and police (may be dissuaded from filing charges against the abuser); know the difficulties of single parenting; know that the abusive spouse controls finances and other necessary resources; does not know about or have access to help and safety; fear not being able to make it on their own; fear losing custody of the children; distrust the legal system and lack adequate police protection; have the mindset that their identity and worth is contingent on being married and it's their responsibility to make the relationship work.

5.   **Victims, abusers, teen**

Exercise Five:

SELF-CHECK

Talk About It!

This exercise is private and not intended to be shared with the group; however, make it clear to members that you are available to speak with anyone who may be in an abusive relationship and need assistance.

On a scale of 4 to 1 (with 4 being "Always" and 1 being "Never"), rate how often you encounter the situations below. These "red flags" are warning signs that danger is imminent. If any of these statements describe your situation, find a way to contact local authorities and/or seek medical attention. The problem will not go away simply because you choose to ignore or minimize it. Your life is too precious for you not to get help.

> **4 = Always   3 = Frequently   2 = Rarely   1 = Never**

Do you:

1.   Experience bouts of depression?   4 3 2 1

2.   Visit hospitals or clinics frequently?   4 3 2 1

3.   Remain isolated from family and friends?   4 3 2 1

4.   Have noticeable bruises, teeth or burn marks, or   4 3 2 1
      have broken bones?

5.   Make excuses for your injuries or cover them up with   4 3 2 1
      clothing and makeup?

6.   Refuse to seek medical attention for fear of angering   4 3 2 1
      your spouse and making the situation worse?

7.   Make excuses for your spouse's violent outbursts?   4 3 2 1

8.   Miss work due to the nature of your injuries?   4 3 2 1

9.   Uncharacteristically use drugs or alcohol?   4 3 2 1

10.   Think or talk about suicide or have attempted suicide?   4 3 2 1

Exercise Six:

FIRING "DOCTOR FEEL GOOD"

Substance abuse is "the overindulgence in, and dependence on, an addictive substance, especially alcohol or a narcotic drug." It is also called *chemical abuse*. By learning what it is, how it develops, its short and long-term effects and how to break out of an addiction, you stand a better chance of keeping your family out of harm's way.

Using chapter 33 as a guide, match the drugs in Column B with their descriptions in Column A. Answers can be used more than once. When you are finished, compare your answers with the answer key at the back of this guide.

<u>Column A</u>	<u>Column B</u>
1.____ Nicotine is in this drug class.	A. Opiates
2.____ This drug class slows the brain's normal operation. It slurs speech, impairs judgement and creates mood swings.	B. CNS Stimulants
3.____ Includes Heroin, Opium, Codeine, Morphine and Demerol.	C. CNS Depressants
4.____ The plant that produces hashish and marijuana.	D. Cannabis

5._____ Has a street name of *Liquid Ecstasy.*   E. Hallucinogens

6._____ *Crank, Meth, Crystal, Coke* are some of   F. Nicotine
its street names.

7._____ Mouth and throat cancer are possible   G. Caffeine
side-effects.

8._____ Peyote, LSD, and PCP are common   H. Inhalants
names for it.

9._____ *Reds, Yellows, Blues, Barb and Downers*
are some of its street names.

10.____ This drug class builds tolerance.

Talk About It!

Using chapter 33, Substance Abuse, as a guide, review the correct answers below. Invite students to participate in an honest discussion regarding past drug use/experimentation or any substance abuse that may be prevalent in their families. You may also wish to set aside class time to view the following films: *Clean and Sober*, *28 Days* and *When a Man Loves a Woman.*

1) B – CNS Stimulants   6) B – CNS Stimulants

2) C – CNS Depressants   7) D – Cannabis

3) A – Opiates   8) E – Hallucinogens

4) D – Cannabis   9) C – CNS Depressants

5) E – Hallucinogens   10) A – Opiates

Exercise Seven:

THE ROAD TO HOOKEDVILLE

Substance abuse becomes habitual through a four-stage process.
Identify which stage corresponds with the statements below.

Experimental Use • Social Use • Chemical Dependency • Chronic Chemical Dependency

---

1. Addiction develops. You no longer have to be with others to get high or drunk. _____

2. In this stage, you *plan* the use of certain substances._____
   _____

3. The abuser uses drugs to feel normal and to avoid withdrawal symptoms. _____

4. You drink and get high on a very limited basis, such as weekend parties. _____

5. You rearrange you routine to accommodate the use of drugs. Denial grows and you refuse to accept that you have a problem.
   _____

6. You make getting high a priority over everything and everyone, and you violate your morals just to get a "fix."
   _____.

7. Some say when people reach this stage, they will remain dependent on drugs for the rest of their lives. _____.

8. At this stage, you create certain boundaries or rules, and *purposefully* seek a "buzz" from liquor or a high from using drugs.

_____

9. Sometimes the person loses control and gets drunk when he really did not plan to, or breaks the rules he established. _____.

10. Tolerance develops and you require more of the drug to achieve the same results as before._____.

Talk About It!

Using the section titled, "Stages of Substance Abuse" in chapter 33 as a guide, review the answers below. In addition, ask those who have overcome a dependency on drugs to share their experience with the rest of the group. You may also wish to attend an AA (Alcoholics Anonymous), NA (Narcotics Anonymous) or Al-Anon/Alateen (for families and friends of alcoholics) meeting for observation purposes.

1) Chemical Dependency   6) Chronic Chemical Dependency

2) Social Use   7) Chronic Chemical Dependency

3) Chronic Chemical Dependency   8) Social Use

4) Experimental Use   9) Chemical Dependency

5) Chemical Dependency   10) Social Use

Exercise Eight:

THE SIGNS DON'T LIE

Talk About It!

Encourage group members to watch their children, spouses or other relatives and friends for the indicators of drug use listed below. Be sure to warn them not to jump the gun too early, as some of these "indicators" may simply be emotional changes common to most adolescents.

The following warning signs are not all-inclusive; but they are common among potential drug users. If you or someone you know is exhibiting any of these behaviors, seek help immediately.

PHYSICAL	SCHOLASTIC / JOB-RELATED
❏ Fatigue ❏ Health complaints ❏ Bloodshot or "glassy" eyes ❏ Chronic cough	❏ Decreased interest in activities, assignments or projects ❏ Negative attitude ❏ Decline in grades/ work performance ❏ Many absences or truancies Disciplinary problems
EMOTIONAL	**SOCIAL**
❏ Personality changes ❏ Mood swings ❏ Irresponsible behavior ❏ Low self-esteem ❏ Poor judgment ❏ Depression and apathy	❏ Has new friends ❏ Loss of interest in favorite activities ❏ Problems with the law ❏ Bizarre way of dressing ❏ Changed interest in music
FAMILY	
❏ Starts arguments ❏ Breaks family rules without caring ❏ Withdrawn and sullen	

Exercise Nine:

FREEDOM IN TRUTH

Read each statement and determine whether it is true (T) or false (F). When you are finished, compare your answers to the answer key at the back of this guide.

1. There is no such thing as an incurable disease.   T   F

2. Inconsistency is the key to breakthrough.   T   F

3. It is possible to live drug and alcohol free.   T   F

4. A counselor who tells you that you need to stop "using"   T   F
    is giving you all the truth you need.

5. The battle against using drugs will be fought in the arena   T   F
    of your mind.

6. *Lavishness* means "unrestrained behavior."   T   F

7. Your flesh is at its weakest when your spirit dominates.   T   F

8. Setting boundaries is a key factor in stopping drug and   T   F
    alcohol abuse.

9. Confessions are God's way of helping you align your   T   F
    thoughts and words with His thoughts and Word.

10. The best thing you can do for an addict is to let him   T   F
    suffer so he can learn his lesson.

Talk About It!

1. **True**

There is no such thing as an irreversible disease. With God, *all things* are possible.

2. **False**

Consistency is the key to breakthrough. When you are consistent about living drug-free, you develop a determination, or a "dogged-ness." People with determination obtain positive, long-lasting results and experience breakthrough in every area of life.

3. **True**

As stated above, nothing is impossible with God. When you do your part (i.e., purpose to live clean), He will do His (add His ability to yours).

4. **False**

Counselors can talk to you all day long, but it takes a consistent effort and a *quality decision* on your part to be free of addiction. If you truly desire to overcome your addiction, renew your mind through the daily reading, study and application of God's Word to your situation.

5. **True**

Keep in mind that you are what you *think* (Proverbs 23:7). Part of the process of renewing your mind involves realizing the physical, emotional and mental damage that drug and alcohol abuse causes.

6. False

The Bible refers to *lasciviousness* as "unrestrained behavior." Think back to the stages of substance abuse. Experimenting with drugs and alcohol can eventually lead to chronic chemical dependence.

7. True

The Word of God says that lasciviousness is a "work of the flesh," or a product of sinful human nature (Galatians 5:19). Your flesh, or soul (the place where your mind, will and emotions reside), is at its *strongest* when it is dominating your spirit. Therefore, it stands to reason that your flesh is at its *weakest* when your spirit dominates. That's why Galatians 5:16 says if you walk (live) by your spirit, you won't fulfill the desires of your flesh.

8. True

Set boundaries and stick to them. Allow the Word of God to define those boundaries. When you trespass those boundaries, you open the door for addiction to creep into your life (Ephesians 4:27). By enforcing your boundaries, you become proficient at resisting temptation.

9. True

Proverbs 18:21 says that you can speak life or death into any situation. God wants you to speak life over yourself daily. Don't confess that you *are* the very thing you from which you are working to free yourself; instead, speak as if you've *already* been delivered from substance abuse.

10. False

Often an abuser may want to break free but does not know where to get help. That's where you come in. Increase your knowledge base about substance abuse so you can effectively help users overcome their addictions.

Exercise Ten:

SPEAK YOUR FREEDOM

Talk About It!

You may assign this exercise as class work or homework. Once group members have completed the assignment, read each scripture aloud and ask members to share what they have written. Review the importance of mind renewal in breaking free of addictions.

Confessing the Word of God daily is a means of building a defense system against the flesh—the sinful part of human nature—so you can overcome substance abuse. Speaking the Word builds your confidence in God's ability to empower you to live alcohol and drug-free.

Look up and write down the scriptures below, inserting your name or need in the verses to make them personal. Speak these scriptures aloud at least 10-20 times a day. Decide once and for all to change the way you *think* and *speak* so you can change the way you *live*.

John 8:31-32

_____

_____

_____

_____

1 Corinthians 10:13

_____

_____

_____

_____

Galatians 5:1

_____

_____

_____

_____

James 4:7

_____

_____

_____

_____

Romans 12:1-2

_____

_____

_____

_____

_____

Exercise Eleven:

SUICIDE IS NOT AN OPTION

Talk About It!

Although this exercise is self-explanatory, remind the group of the importance of allowing emotions to run their course and the danger associated with repressing them. In addition, explain how recording and sharing their triumphs and tragedies, whether great or small, can help them to release pent-up emotions and remind them of God's goodness on difficult days.

Depression and suicide are epidemics that touch the lives of thousands of people every year. Throughout the course of your life, you will encounter a number of situations that may tempt you to give up, cave in and quit. Keep in mind, however, that quitting is never a valid option.

If you or someone you know is or has ever contemplated suicide, take heart. Although depression and suicide are the results of an empty spirit and untamed emotions, you can turn these weaknesses into strengths. Begin to see yourself and your future through God's eyes. You are a priceless treasure to Him, and He has a great plan for your life. Experience His love so that you may live life to the fullest.

To help you overcome depression and suicidal tendencies, purchase a journal or scrapbook and use it as a creative outlet for your emotions.

- Write down what you're thinking and feeling daily.

- Review what you have written and measure it against what the Word of God has to say about what you were feeling and experiencing at the time.

- Make a list of things you are thankful for or the things in life you love the most.

- Add drawings, photos or magazine cutouts to illustrate your innermost desires.

When you are depressed, take out your journal or scrapbook and review its contents for encouragement. In addition, take the time to pray and hear what God wants to speak to your heart. You may also ask God for a specific plan on how you can live free of depression. Write it down and begin to implement it.

Exercise Twelve:

THE ROAD SIGNS OF DEPRESSION

Talk About It!

Encourage group members to examine their lives (or that of someone they know) for signs of depression. If anyone has experienced three or more of these symptoms for more than a week, assist that individual in seeking adequate counseling.

This exercise will help you to determine if you or someone you know is suffering from depression. Read each statement below and answer Yes of No. If six or more of these symptoms have lasted for more than two weeks, it's time to get help.

1.	Fatigue and loss of energy	**Yes**	**No**
2.	Little or no emotional control (severe mood swings) or emotional "numbness"	**Yes**	**No**
3.	Weight loss or weight gain	**Yes**	**No**
4.	Continuous illness or symptoms of disease	**Yes**	**No**
5.	Unable to think clearly or make decisions	**Yes**	**No**
6.	Restlessness or apathy	**Yes**	**No**

7.	Uncharacteristic use of drugs and/or alcohol	**Yes**	**No**
8.	Insomnia or sleeping too much	**Yes**	**No**
9.	Loss of interest in hobbies, sports and other enjoyable activities	**Yes**	**No**
10.	Neglect of personal hygiene	**Yes**	**No**
11.	Feelings of guilt, hopelessness or worthlessness	**Yes**	**No**
12.	Overly critical of self	**Yes**	**No**
13.	Loss of sexual drive	**Yes**	**No**
14.	Hurts others with behavior	**Yes**	**No**
15.	Preoccupation with suicide and death	**Yes**	**No**

Exercise Thirteen:

SUICIDE WATCH

Talk About It!

This exercise is similar to exercise 12 in that it requires your group to face the facts about depression and suicidal behavior. Using chapter 34, *Suicide and Depression,* as a guide, discuss each symptom listed below, and ask group members if they or anyone they know has tried to commit suicide. Focus on who or what prevented them from doing so.

Have you noticed a change of behavior or attitude in a loved one, friend or co-worker? At first, it may seem as if he or she might be slightly depressed or upset about something and is unable to get over it. If you suspect that this person might be contemplating suicide, don't panic. Read each statement below and answer Yes or No for each. When you have finished, review your answers. If more "yes" answers have been circled, seek professional help immediately.

1.	Suddenly giving away prized possessions	**Yes**	**No**
2.	Trouble eating, sleeping or concentrating	**Yes**	**No**

3.	Preoccupied with death and dying	**Yes**	**No**
4.	Loss of interest in hobbies, work, school or other social activities	**Yes**	**No**
5.	Preoccupied with getting his/her "house in order"	**Yes**	**No**
6.	Shows a lack of interest in the future	**Yes**	**No**
7.	Is convinced that the world will be better off if he/she were not around	**Yes**	**No**
8.	Loss of interest in personal hygiene	**Yes**	**No**
9.	Daring or high-risk behavior	**Yes**	**No**
10.	Drastic changes in personality (i.e., withdrawal or aggression)	**Yes**	**No**

The following are guidelines that will assist you in reaching out to a suicidal individual.

- Take threats of suicide seriously
- Show concern and a desire to help
- Be available to listen
- Ask questions
- Don't be judgmental
- Get professional help even if the person tells you not to
- Do not leave the person alone
- Do not promise not to tell anyone

Exercise Fourteen:

FINDING THE ANSWER

Talk About It!

This exercise is designed to be a source of encouragement for people who are depressed and/or suicidal. Encourage group members to keep this sheet handy in order to help anyone they know who may be struggling with depression due to loss or a misfortune.

When a person looks to things or people to satisfy a void in his life, the result will be disappointment and devastation. When his source of dependence is removed, he is unable to cope with the stresses of life.

Most people fall into depression or have suicidal thoughts because their ability to cope is small in comparison to daily pressure or other losses they may experience. When you sense that you have an inability to cope with a challenge, look to the Lord for strength. He is the answer to every dilemma.

The scriptures listed below will help you in times of need if you study them. Take the time to meditate on them daily until those negative or self-depreciating thoughts are completely eradicated from your life.

- Psalm 22:19; 27:1; 30:10; 33:20; 37:39-40; 40:17; 46:5; 59:9; 63:7-8; 70:1; 71:12; 72:12; 105:4; 109:26; 119:173; 121:1-2

- 1 Samuel 30:6

- Isaiah 40:29; 41:10, 13-14; 50:7

- Mark 9:23-24

- Hebrews 13:6

Exercise Fifteen:

A SUCCESSFUL COUNTERATTACK

Below are typical thoughts that allow depression to remain in an individual's life. When he or she attempts to fight these negative thoughts with thoughts, the battle will be lost. The war against depression is won by implementing a sound counterattack with words—more specifically with God's Word.

Use these scriptures to defeat depressive thoughts. Write down what these passages mean to you. Feel free to include other verses that specifically minister to your situation. Study them until they become ingrained in your heart. Remember to speak them in faith.

Talk About It!

Instruct the group to carefully consider the following questions and then answer them in the spaces provided. When everyone has finished, discuss what the Word has to say about living depression-free. Provide members with the additional scripture references found after each discussion point.

---

1.   Thought: *"I don't think I can make it without him or her."*
     Truth: Isaiah 43:2; Philippians 4:3

What do these scriptures mean to me?_____
_____
_____
_____

Psalm 3:3; Deuteronomy 1:30; Philippians 1:6; Psalm 23:6; John 14:18

2.   Thought: *"It seems like I'm never going to get out of all this debt."*
     Truth: Philippians 4:19; Luke 6:38

What do these scriptures mean to me?_____
_____
_____
_____

Jeremiah 33:3; 1 Peter 5:7; Psalm 91:14-15

3.   Thought: *"It feels like I'm in this world all by myself."*
     Truth: Isaiah 49:15-16; Deuteronomy 31:6

What do these scriptures mean to me?_____
_____
_____
_____

> Psalm 94:14; Deuteronomy 4:31; Isaiah 41:17

4.   Thought: *"I don't think anybody really loves me."*
       Truth: Romans 8:38-39; Jeremiah 31:3; Zechariah 2:8

What do these scriptures mean to me?_____

_____

_____

_____

> John 17:26; 1 Corinthians 13:7, AMP; 1 John 4:7-9, 16-18

5.   Thought: *"It seems as though I'm a total failure."*
       Truth: Isaiah 40:29; Isaiah 41:10; Isaiah 50:7

What do these scriptures mean to me?_____

_____

_____

_____

> Psalm 31:24; Isaiah 40:31; Philippians 4:13

6.   Thought: *"It seems that the only way to peace is death."*
       Truth: Psalm 118:17; Romans 8:6; John 14:27

What do these scriptures mean to me?_____

_____

_____

_____

Isaiah 26:3; Romans 5:1; Philippians 4:7

---

7.   Thought: _____
     Truth:_____

What do these scriptures mean to me?_____

_____

_____

_____

8.   Thought: _____
     Truth:_____

What do these scriptures mean to me?_____

_____

_____

_____

Exercise Sixteen:

KICKING THE BINGE

Talk About It!

When everyone has completed the exercise, discuss why answering *yes* to any of these statements could indicate the potential for, or presence of, an eating disorder. Solicit responses on what are healthy ways to perceive oneself versus the world's "supermodel" ideal. As you begin discussing this subject, be sensitive to those who may find it difficult to share their experiences. Pay attention to the mood of the group as you go over each statement.

Eating disorders are the result of distorted self-perception. Often the individual compares herself to a standard image that society deems beautiful. He or she forgets, however, that everyone's genetic makeup is unique, and that what works for one person may not work for another.

The key to overcoming an eating disorder is conforming oneself to the image set forth in the Word of God. An individual must first admit there is a problem, and then develop and implement a sound plan of action based on scripture. To determine if you have a distorted view of yourself physically, read each statement below and circle Yes or No.

1.	I constantly complain about my weight.	**Yes**	**No**
2.	I constantly compare myself to "supermodel" standards of perfection.	**Yes**	**No**
3.	My family and friends are concerned about my weight.	**Yes**	**No**
4.	My family and friends are concerned about my current fitness program.	**Yes**	**No**
5.	Each time I look in the mirror, I look fatter and fatter.	**Yes**	**No**
6.	I am never pleased with how I look physically.	**Yes**	**No**
7.	I feel fat no matter how little I eat.	**Yes**	**No**
8.	I'm fearful of ingesting too much fat or too many calories	**Yes**	**No**
9.	I believe that food is my enemy.	**Yes**	**No**
10.	I have frequent episodes of uncontrolled overeating.	**Yes**	**No**

If you answered yes to any of these questions, seek help from a parent, friend, counselor, minister, teacher, doctor or eating disorder organization. Discuss your fears or concerns with whomever you choose, but don't neglect to adjust your thinking so you can see your true inner and outer beauty.

Exercise Seventeen:

ERASING THE "DIS" FROM DISORDER

Listed below are several basic facts about eating disorders. Increase your knowledge base concerning these unhealthy habits by match the disorder with its basic fact. Refer to chapter 35 in *The Successful Family* to learn more. Use the answer key at the end of this guide to find the correct answers.

Anorexia Nervosa	•	**Bulimia Nervosa**	•	**Binge Eating**

1. This condition is characterized by frequent episodes of uncontrolled overeating, but does not involve purging. _____

2. Occurs in individuals who secretly engage in a cycle of binge eating followed by purging._____

3. Occurs when the individual experiences excessive weight loss through self-starvation._____

4. Often these individuals appear to have an average body weight, which makes it easy for their eating disorder behavior to go unnoticed. _____

5. Individuals suffering from this eating disorder, which has an extremely high death rate, refuse to maintain the ideal body weight for their height, body frame and age._____

6. These individuals engage in sporadic fasts or repetitive diets that result in feelings of shame or self-hatred. _____

7. Symptoms of this disorder include a fear of becoming overweight, feeling fat in spite of dramatic weight loss, preoccupation with body weight and shape and loss of menstrual cycle._____

8. This disorder is also known as "Compulsive Overeating."_____

9. Warning signs of this disorder include:

   • The disappearance of large amounts of food in short periods.
   • Frequent trips to the restroom immediately after meals.
   • The smell and signs of vomiting.
   • Swelling in the cheeks or jaws area.
   • Involvement in an excessive and rigid exercise program.

   _____

10. Heart disease, high blood pressure, high cholesterol, secondary diabetes and gallbladder disease are health issues associated with this disorder._____

Talk About It!

Review the correct answers below. Ask whether or not group members have struggled with an eating disorder and if any are willing to share their experiences. To facilitate this discussion, refer to the section in chapter 35 titled, "Just the Facts."

1) **Binge Eating**

2) **Bulimia Nervosa**

3) **Anorexia Nervosa**

4) **Bulimia Nervosa**

5) **Anorexia Nervosa**

6) **Binge Eating**

7) **Anorexia Nervosa**

8) **Binge Eating**

9) **Bulimia Nervosa**

10) **Binge Eating**

REMOVING THE BLINDERS

Oftentimes, warning signs of eating disorders are either ignored or overlooked. Below are warning signs with which you should become familiar. If a friend or relative displays any of these symptoms, take the necessary steps to get them help.

For this exercise, write the disorder in the blank space next to its warning sign. Refer to chapter 35 for more information about these disorders.

Anorexia Nervosa   •   **Bulimia Nervosa**   •   **Binge Eating**

---

1. _____   Frequent trips to the restroom immediately after eating.

2. _____   Hiding food and wrappers; eating in secret.

3. _____   Giving excuses to avoid meals or situations involving food.

4. _____   Drastic weight loss.

5. _____   Swelling in the cheeks or jaw area.

6. _____   Consumption of large amounts of food with out feeling hungry.

7. _____   Continual denial of hunger.

8. _____ Isolation and withdrawal from normal activities.

9. _____ The smell and/or signs of vomiting.

10. _____ Eating rapidly and/or hoarding food.

Talk About It!

Parents can recognize an eating disorder in their children *if* they are aware of the warning signs. Therefore, be sure to thoroughly review the information in this exercise and the correct answers below.

1) **Bulimia Nervosa**

2) **Binge Eating**

3) **Anorexia Nervosa**

4) **Anorexia Nervosa**

5) **Bulimia Nervosa**

6) **Binge Eating**

7) **Anorexia Nervosa**

8) **Anorexia Nervosa**

9) **Bulimia Nervosa**

10) **Binge Eating**

Exercise Nineteen:

FEEL THE PAIN

Below are the harmful physical effects that are a common result of eating disorders. Match the disorders to the effects they produce.

Anorexia Nervosa • Bulimia Nervosa • Binge Eating

1._____The body suffers from dehydration and loss of potassium and sodium.

2._____Gallbladder disease, high cholesterol and high blood pressure.

3._____Heart failure due to slowed heart rate.

4._____Low blood pressure, fainting and fatigue.

5._____Gastric rupture, inflammation and rupture of the esophagus.

6._____Tooth decay and staining from stomach acids.

7._____Muscle loss, osteoporosis and severe dehydration.

8._____Downy layer of hair covers the body for warmth.

9._____Anxiety attacks and depression.

10._____Constipation and chronic irregular bowel movements.

Talk About It!

Review the correct answers with the group.

1) Bulimia Nervosa

2) Binge Eating

3) Anorexia Nervosa

4) Anorexia Nervosa

5) Bulimia Nervosa

6) Bulimia Nervosa

7) Anorexia Nervosa

8) Anorexia Nervosa

9) Binge Eating

10) Bulimia Nervosa

Exercise Twenty:

LEND A HELPING HAND

Talk About It!

This exercise is designed to aid parents and/or adults in handling situations where their children or students may be dealing with eating disorders. For those in the group who have dealt with eating disorders in the past, encourage them to expound on the situation and the ways in which it was handled.

Here are several strategies for eating disorder prevention and/or early intervention. The goal of this exercise is to help you become *proactive* rather than reactive in regard to the physical and mental health of your children.

- Be aware that certain athletic activities, such as gymnastics, often have weight restrictions which may pressure your child into developing an eating disorder.

- Explain to your children the importance of not conforming to the standards of beauty set forth by society through advertisements and other media.

- Confront the parents of those who tease your children about their weight.

- Explain to your children the importance of self-acceptance.

- Teach them the dangers of altering one's shape through excessive dieting.

- Teach your children the value of exercise and nutrition.

- Be a good example for your children by eating sensibly and participating in a regular exercise program.

- If your child is younger than 18 years old and has developed an eating disorder, get professional help immediately. Begin with a trip to your family doctor for a medical exam, then request that he/she refer you to a specialist.

- If your child's friend is younger than 18 years old and exhibits signs of an eating disorder, tell his/her parents about your observations.

Reactive Responses

- Do not waste time trying to assure the person that he/she isn't fat.

- Never say "You're too thin," or "I'm glad that you've gained some weight."

- Do not snoop or pry; instead, respect the person's privacy.

- Do not criticize, shame or attempt to control the person

- Do not discuss counting calories, eating food, diets or proper weight control.

- Do not nag, beg, bribe, threaten or manipulate.

Proactive Responses

- If the person is too scared to see a doctor or counselor alone, go with him/her.

- Be supportive and caring.

- Be a good listener.

- Realize that eating disorders happen because the person feels completely out of control.

- Realize that eating disorders can also occur as a rebuttal to control.

- Voice your concern with gentleness.

- Discuss the advantages of living without starving or bingeing.

- Increase your knowledge of eating disorders and their treatment.

Twenty-One:

DISCIPLINE GONE TOO FAR

When God said to use the rod of correction to drive foolishness out of children (Proverbs 22:15), He was not advocating abuse. Discipline and correction should be based on *love*. Unfortunately, one of the most tragic occurrences is violence against children at the hands of caregivers.

Child abuse can generally be divided into four categories: physical, sexual, emotional/ verbal and neglect. If you recognize any of the following signs of abuse, call local authorities immediately so both the adult and child receive help. Using chapter 36 as a guide, read each statement below and determine whether it is true (T) or false (F). When you are finished, compare your answers with the answer key at the back of this guide.

1. Child abuse is one of the leading causes of death in young children.   **T F**

2. At times the child may deny any maltreatment and make excuses for his injuries.   **T F**

3. Emotional abuse is not easily detected.   **T F**

4. The most common form of child abuse is neglect.   **T F**

5. If abused as children, the victims are at a high risk of becoming abusers themselves.   **T F**

6. Older children who are abused find it difficult   T   F
   to form close ties with others.

7. Abused teenagers often commit delinquent acts,   T   F
   which may later develop into more serious criminal
   activity.

8. Most abusers are former victims of abuse who had   T   F
   insecure, fearful and dangerous relationships with
   their own parents.

9. Neighbors should get involved in situations where   T   F
   child abuse is suspected, whether it's direct intervention
   or by contacting local authorities.

10. Acts of abuse are merely the manifestation of a deeper,   T   F
    more serious condition existing on the inside.

Talk About It!

Review the answers below. Be sure to discuss with the group the four main types of child abuse, as well as the common behaviors of abused children and their abusers.

1. True

Best described as "intentional acts resulting in physical or emotional harm," *child abuse* is one of the leading causes of death in young children. Thousands of children are killed each year and thousands more suffer permanent physical, mental and emotional damage.

2. **True**

Experts believe that child abuse is the most unreported crime due to fear and a "code of silence" that often exists.

3. **True**

This type of abuse affects the character and self-esteem of a child, and rarely has any physical signs aside from a negative change in demeanor and countenance.

4. **True**

The failure of a caregiver to adequately provide for a child's basic needs constitutes physical neglect. Other areas include improper supervision and protection from hazardous materials and dangerous situations. Neglect can also come in the form of educational neglect where a child is allowed to skip school, or the caregiver fails to enroll him or her in school.

5. **True**

Abuse is a *learned* behavior; therefore, victims of abuse are at high risk for becoming abusers themselves. In addition, psychiatric disorders like depression, excessive anxiety or Multiple Personality Disorder may develop. There is also an increased risk of suicide among the more severe cases.

6.   True

Most abused infants, toddlers and preschoolers display insecure attachments to others, while older children find it difficult to form close ties.

7.   True

Often, this is an act of rebellion against the very system (parenthood) that is supposed to protect children. Abused teenagers have so much bottled anger that they may choose to release it by committing criminal acts.

8.   True

Most abusers are former victims of abuse who had insecure, fearful and/or dangerous relationships with their own parents. They were not taught how to form warm, secure family ties, which adversely affects their *own* family. This is known as a *generational curse*—a destructive action that is passed from one generation to the next.

9.   True

To ignore the evidence of child abuse, whether in your home or that of other family, is no different than condoning the act. We all have a responsibility to protect the lives of children, regardless of whether or not they are our own.

10. True

Often abusers are only counseled/treated on a superficial level, while the root cause of their abusive behavior is rarely exposed and destroyed.

Exercise Twenty-Two:

MENDING BROKEN PIECES

Best described as "intentional acts resulting in physical or emotional harm," *child abuse* is one of the leading causes of death among young children. Thousands of children are killed each year and thousands more suffer permanent physical, mental and emotional damage.

Child abuse should not be taken lightly. Your intervention may save the life of a child—even your own. You can start intervening by completing this exercise, which is designed to highlight the truth about violence against children. Using chapter 36 as a guide, complete the sentences by writing the correct answers in the spaces provided. Once you have finished, compare your answers with the answer key at the end of this guide.

1.   Child abuse can generally be divided into four categories: _____, _____ _____, _____

2.   _____ is the type of abuse that involves deliberate acts of violence in an effort to wound or kill.

3.   _____ is the type of abuse also known as *pedophilia*.

4. The type of abuse characterized by acts of verbal and mental mal-treatment is referred to as _____ _____.

5. Acts of _____ include allowing the child to skip school and not providing for a special educational need.

6. According to researchers, child abuse generally stems from the following four influences: _____, _____ and _____ forces, and _____.

Talk About It!

Using chapter 36, *Child Abuse*, review the following answers with the group.

1) **Physical, sexual, emotional/verbal, neglect**

2) **Physical abuse**

3) **Sexual abuse against children**

4) **Emotional abuse**

5) **Educational neglect**

6) **Poverty, social, cultural, isolation**

Exercise Twenty-Three:

GETTING THE SCOOP ON ABUSE

Talk About It!

Use the information in the following exercises to facilitate a discussion on the subject of child abuse. Be prepared to answer questions.

The following exercise is designed to help you increase your knowledge base of *physical* child abuse. Review the information and be prepared to discuss what you've read with a partner or the rest of your group.

Examples:
- Maliciously beating, kicking or hitting of a child using any object
- Breaking a child's bones
- Burning a child with an iron, matches or cigarettes
- Not letting a child eat, drink or use the bathroom
- Pulling a child's hair violently
- Scalding a child with hot water
- Shaking, shoving and slapping

Indicators:
- Bruises or welts on the body or face
- Burn or bite marks
- Fractures

- Internal injuries
- Lacerations and abrasions, especially around the mouth, eyes or genitalia

Child's Behavior:

Agitation

Anger and rage

Anxiety or fears

Apprehension when other children cry

Avoids social contact or seems withdrawn

Behaves aggressively

Changes in behavior or school performance

Cries frequently

Demonstrates extremes in behavior

Destroys or throws objects

Nightmares

Poor self-image

Sadness

Seems afraid of a parent or other adults

Startles easily

Tired often

Wary of physical contact with adults

Depression

Alcohol or drug abuse

Fights with other children

Flashbacks, shock

Hard to believe stories of injuries

Immature behaviors (i.e. thumb-sucking)

Lies frequently

Loitering for fear of going home

Passive or withdrawn behavior

Reports injury by parents

School problems

Self-destructive behavior

Suicidal preoccupation

Stealing

Trouble sleeping

Caretaker's Behavior:

- Uses inappropriate harsh discipline
- Unrealistic expectations of the child
- Offers illogical, unconvincing and contradictory explanations of the child's injury
- Seems unconcerned about the child's welfare
- Exhibits psychotic behavior
- Abuses alcohol or other drugs
- Attempts to conceal child's injury

Exercise Twenty-Four:

WHO'S WATCHING LITTLE JOHNNY?

The following exercise presents the facts about *child neglect* and how it can be detected. Review the information and be prepared to discuss it with a partner or others in your group.

Examples:
- Not meeting the child's basic needs (i.e., clothing, nutrition, adequate shelter and affection)
- Leaving the child unsupervised for extended periods
- Leaving the child in an unsafe environment
- Not seeking necessary medical and dental attention for the child
- Not permitting the child to attend school
- Not seeking special services for children in need of educational support

Child's Appearance and Behavior:
- Abuses alcohol and other drugs
- Begs for or steals food
- Consistently dirty, hungry or inappropriately dressed
- Constantly fatigued or listless
- Engages in dangerous activities
- Engages in delinquent acts
- Is exploited or overworked
- Lacks adult supervision
- Lacks treatment for medical conditions or dental care
- Loses weight or fails to gain weight

- Requires eye glasses, but never receives them
- Skips or misses school frequently

Caretaker's Behavior:
- Misuses alcohol or other drugs
- Maintains chaotic home life
- Shows evidence of apathy or futility
- Is mentally ill or of diminished intelligence
- Has history of neglect as a child
- Overly self-absorbed

Exercise Twenty-Five:

EMOTIONAL ROLLER COASTER

Similar to exercises 23 and 24, this exercise will assist you in knowing more about abuse—in this case, *emotional abuse*. Review the information below and be prepared to discuss what you have read.

Examples:
- Antisocial behavior
- Belittling the child or inhibiting the child's potential
- Coldness or indifference
- Cruelty
- Extreme inconsistency
- Harassment and repeated exposure to fear
- Ignoring the child
- Inappropriate control
- Isolating or sheltering the child from normal social contact
- Negating the child's self-image
- Terrorizing and repeatedly igniting a stress response in the child
- Withholding essential stimulation and interaction

Child's Behavior:
- Appears overly compliant, passive and apathetic
- Appears very anxious or depressed
- Attempts suicide
- Avoids doing things with other children
- Behaves immaturely

- Has difficulty socializing
- Exhibits extremely aggressive, demanding or enraged behavior
- Lags in physical, emotional and intellectual development
- Wets or soils the bed

Caretaker's Behavior:

- Blames or belittles the child
- Is cold and rejecting
- Seems unconcerned about child's welfare
- Treats siblings unequally
- Withholds love

Exercise Twenty-Six:

TRACKING A PEDOPHILE

This final exercise will provide you with information regarding *sexual abuse* and will help you recognize the warning signs. Review this information thoroughly and share your thoughts with a partner or other group members.

Examples:
- Finger penetration
- Exhibitionism
- Fondling a child's genitals
- Intercourse with a child (sodomy)
- Oral sex with a child
- Sex in front of a child
- Making a child touch an older person's genitals
- Incest
- Masturbation
- Prostitution
- Rape
- Showing X-rated books or movies to a child
- Using a child in a pornographic production

Child's Appearance:

- Has torn, stained, or bloody underclothing
- Experiences pain or itching in the genital area
- Has bruises in or around genitalia or anal region
- Has a sexually transmitted disease
- Has swollen or red cervix, vulva or perineum
- Has semen around mouth, genitalia or on clothing
- Is pregnant

Child's Behavior:

- Appears withdrawn or engages in fantasy or infantile behavior
- Begins wetting or soiling bed
- Lack of peer relationships
- Is unwilling to participate in physical activities
- Is engaging in delinquent acts
- Reports sexual abuse
- Engages in inappropriate sexualized behavior
- Devalues sexual acts
- Fears a certain person or place
- Has an unreasonable fear of a physical exam
- Creates drawings that show sexual acts or sexual body parts
- More knowledge about sex than is normal for the child's age
- Pain, bruising or bleeding in the genitals
- Responds unusually when asked if touched inappropriately by someone
- Runs away
- Seems preoccupied with or overly concerned about sex and sexual language

Caretaker's Behavior:

- Extremely protective or jealous of child
- Encourages child to engage in prostitution or sexual acts
- Has been sexually abused as a child
- Is experiencing marital difficulties
- Abuses alcohol or other drugs
- Is frequently absent from home
- Has difficulty in interacting emotionally with other adults

NOTES

NOTES

NOTES

NOTES

NOTES